THE GREEN TUXEDO

THE ERNEST SANDEEN PRIZE IN POETRY

EDITOR
John Matthias

1999, *The Green Tuxedo,* Janet Holmes
1997, *True North,* Stephanie Strickland

THE GREEN TUXEDO

Janet Holmes

University of Notre Dame Press
Notre Dame, Indiana

Published by
University of Notre Dame Press
Notre Dame, Indiana 46556
All Rights Reserved

Manufactured in the United States of America

Library of Congress Cataloging-in-Publication Data

Holmes, Janet (Janet A.)
    The green tuxedo / Janet Holmes.
        p.   cm. — (The Ernest Sandeen prize in poetry)
    ISBN 0-268-01036-6 (alk. paper)
    I. Title.   II. Series.
PS3558.035935G74   1998
811'.54—dc21   97-32925
                                                              CIP

∞ *The paper used in this publication meets the minimum requirements of the
American National Standard for Information Sciences—Permanence of
Paper for Printed Library Materials, ANSI Z39.48-1984.*

For Al

CONTENTS

ACKNOWLEDGMENTS

Grateful acknowledgment is made to the following publications, in which some of these poems have appeared:

The Beloit Poetry Journal ("The Blue World")
Blue Moon ("Still Life with Bad Dog")
The Carolina Quarterly ("The Green Tuxedo")
Crania ("Your Bird," "Florida, 1985," "My Mother's Clown")
The Georgia Review ("Against the Literal," "Departures")
Michigan Quarterly Review ("The Duck at Midlife")
Notre Dame Review ("Yellow Period," "At Tea with the Epistemologist," "The Bachelor's House")
Passages North ("Post-Solstice")
Poetry ("The Erotics of Detail")
Seneca Review ("The Aquarium")

"Against the Literal" appeared in *The Best American Poetry 1995*.
"The Bachelor's House," "The Blue World," "Florida, 1985," "My Mother's Clown," and "Why" appeared in *Gravity's Loophole*. St. Paul, Minn.: The Loft, 1997.

Thanks to the Minnesota State Arts Board and the Bush Foundation for grants of support while these poems were being written.

Notes

"Against the Literal" is for Alvin Greenberg.
"Yellow Period": Lines in section three are from "Long and Sluggish Lines," by Wallace Stevens. A *bulto* is a freestanding wooden carved figure.

"The Green Tuxedo": Russell Smith of Santa Fe originally told me about the
    Amos 'n' Andy exchange, for which I thank him.

"Hieroglyphs": the artist John Himmelfarb and his work play important parts
    in this poem.

The sequence "The Time Savers" is for my mother, Miriam O'May Holmes.

"Who" contains fragments from the *Chicago Tribune* obituary of Paul A.
    Holmes by Kenan Heise, published on January 15, 1985.

"Radio Interview" refers to an NPR interview of Iris Dement aired during
    January 1995.

The Green Tuxedo

Against the Literal

Of course each shrub and rodent has a name, sometimes more than one,
and every weed and every flower and all the sonorous trees,

and the winds too, their mistrals and sciroccos and easts and wests,
but I am telling you to keep them from me a moment: if the gray jay

and the pinyon jay are the same, I don't need to know yet,
and I most want to be rid of Latin binomials. We are entering

new country. If I see the same squirrel five times, must I know
there is one peripatetic, curious little animal, or may I believe

the woods are teeming with squirrels? The sun is brighter
here than anywhere else: I don't care if the altitude provides a logical

explanation; it's brighter just now for other reasons. Observe:
the flowers here have more seductive fragrances. If I were to think

your voice carries especially far because I always hear it,
or that the camp robber takes bread from my hand for reasons other

than greed, would it trouble you not to disabuse me? I'm not saying
forever. Long enough. A moment.

Yellow Period

—that winter driving sixty dull miles
to work every day, sixty anxious miles back,
falling out of love: the odometer rolling each new number
relentlessly up, a taunt:
now? Now?
and from the radio nothing but the war:
live, up-to-the-minute reports. On Main Street
a storefront festooned itself with yellow bows,
and a second followed suit, and a few houses
hung them from their doors like holiday wreaths.
Ribbons streamed out from car antennae. At five o'clock
in Minnesota's pearl twilight, they were beacons,
advertisements for unrequited love . . .
She viewed them from the streaked windshield
as if witnessing a doomed wedding:
the bride devoted and ignorant, the angry groom
smirking behind his champagne during the feast—

—————————

Quarter the lemons—
                                        not all the way through
but so they open out to you, as a bud
unfurls itself in stop-motion, as the mouths
of chicks clamor upwards from the nest: pour salt
into the cloven fruit, and layer them
in a wide-mouthed jar, letting
fresh juice seep into the interstices.
Take care that the jar closes tightly:
each day invert it, and wait—

after a month you will have
preserved lemons to eat,
but all that time you will have the jar

yellow in your kitchen, a bottle
of fractured suns
half the time on its head,
uncynical, brilliant—

———————————

What opposite? Could it be that yellow patch,
the side of a house, that makes one think the house is laughing?

———————————

In the adobe church, candles gutter before the *bulto*
of *Nuestra Señora de los Dolores,*
                              a supernatural strobe effect:
the pale buttery halo around the saint
slightly unreliable—
                    her face now in shadow,
now lit and upturned, the eyes immeasurably sad.

———————————

Caution lights lining the highway (forever?)
        —at least to the vanishing point, sliding along a curve
starting up the mountain, flashing their amber badges
every second; it was like (every second)
waking up from a dream: she shouldn't be driving:
she could imagine shattering the rail,
sending the car over, regretting it,
clutching the plastic wheel:
seeing the glowing disks, the last things—
(Later, in town, sweating:
she had pulled herself up there hand over hand
by the yellow lines in the road . . .)

5

Winter light in the afternoon.
Gainsborough's sky here in Minnesota,
nominally blue, but with a yellow glaze in the west:
aged overpainting,
oily and glistening, giving the clouds portent—
giving portent, rather, to the billowing steam
rising grand from the taconite plant
and drifting, pompous, over the icy lake—

Taxi! Taxi!
Yeah, get me out of here, let's move it—

At Tea with the Epistemologist

Leaves of Darjeeling, and china
of regrettable fragility: "Out of sight," she says,
"out of mind," and pours. This is not
our ceremony. The sentence hangs between us,
translatable:
> *As soon as I don't see him,*
I forget him. Sugar is proffered
with silverplate tongs. *As soon as I can't*
see him, I stop thinking. If he
cannot be seen, I will not think of him.
A spin of milk loses itself in the cup.
Can't see him anymore,
can't think of him anymore;
when I don't see him, I can't think . . .
If I can't see him,
I won't remember him. He's hidden;
he is thoughtless. I won't see him,
she tells me, I'll forget him.
He is gone, so my mind is a blank.
He is blind, and he must be crazy.

The Duck at Midlife

In a few seconds it will start the path again, left to right,
the smiling tin duck with its enormous, childlike eyes
and a head nearly as big as its body, but now it rides upside-down
in the gallery's rusted underworld; and it does not matter
that the carny hawks plush trophies and hides the impossible odds,
nor that most of the players taking shots
are after different game than this booth offers.
What matters is the circuit, hundreds of times a day, the left-right path;
what matters is the grin-stretched beak touched up each season
with yellow paint where pellets make their dents—

The Blue World

There, says the guidebook, they live
in peace all winter: tunnels glowing glacier-blue

in the short afternoons, the worst predators
gone, gone, gone: it's frozen,

but under the snow a paradise
of shrews, thirteen-lined ground squirrels,

deer mice, voles, who feed for months
on the forest floor. There's no

wind. The air warms
in the narrow channels. Silence.

Silence. True, some scrabble
up to the crusted surface, discontent

with the crystal walls, the delicate
ice-carved rooms. True, the great grey owl

hears its prey through a three-foot snowfall:
slim weasels negotiate the maze:

dangers, even now. A vole
emerging into the winter trail

surprises a lapdog out for its walk,
whose dormant instincts quicken:

who seizes it. Shakes it dead.
Drop it, girl! Good girl! We pass

the fresh crater a squirrel made, having exited
a high branch—

and its quick prints off to a different
safety. So comic: a pratfall!

Here, my love: something to make you laugh.
No, no, I'm happy. Honestly. Light,

filtered and blue, softened, all afternoon
through the cold walls—

Really I am. See, I'm smiling.

The Green Tuxedo

1.
"He reminds me of a man who once sold me a green tuxedo."

2. *Family Values*
The years-long feud between brothers. The incest.
Wife-beating when drunk, or whenever.
They dumped her in a home.
Humiliations. *(You _____!)* Child
molestation. *Nobody's business.* If you didn't flaunt it,
adultery. *Everyone does it.* Faithlessness.
I'm cutting you out of the will.
The local priest, the daycare worker, names
in the paper. *He had his reasons.*
She asked for it.
Dirty linen, they said. The father who left.
The father they never met. *They'll get over it.*
The boy will. Disowning the gay son.
The girl will get married someday, she'll have kids of her own—
What will the neighbors think. The smile forced on.

3.
You thought there was somebody there, but then when you looked, they were gone.
Not even a leaf moving.

4. *From Interviews (St. Paul, 1991)*
It was a pretty small cross.
It wasn't like he shot anybody. Nothing else
caught on fire. It was an expression
of free speech. Are you saying
I don't have rights? I don't, and they do? Maybe

he shouldn't have put it on their lawn. OK, so maybe
next time put it on public land. In the town square.
In front of the jail. In front of the courthouse.
It was only a prank. You know? It was only a joke.
Another thing about them: they can't take a joke.

5. *The Green Tuxedo*

It's Amos 'n' Andy, the old TV show. They're sitting on a porch, and a beauti-
ful fancy car pulls up and parks. A handsome man gets out, and a beautiful,
fancy woman with a big, elegant dog on a leash—perhaps a Russian wolf-
hound—gets out, and they walk slowly past Amos 'n' Andy. Amos turns
to Andy (or was it the other way round?) and says, "He reminds me of a
man who

6.

Meaning, *he sold me something I didn't need?*
Something nobody needs?
Something beautiful but useless?
Something I only wore once?
Something that impressed my lover?
that made me look ridiculous?
that quickly went out of style?
that I never looked at again?
that I buried in the closet?
that I secretly loved?
that shamed me?

7. *World Affairs*

The woman with a son in the Gulf wears his picture
as a button on her jacket. She is accorded some status,
as were women required to breed for the state in Romania.
She hates every boy his age who is not there. She loves

the President. In the video-game war nobody dies.
The soldiers worry that one of them may be gay,
may be watching in the shower—
          and what do the young men in Bosnia fear,
          who every day work in the rape camps?
In the video-game war only nobodies died.
The woman with a son in the Gulf knows
who the enemy is.

8.
turns to him and says, "He reminds me of a man who

9.
Meaning, *he's a questionable character?*
He'll take advantage of me?
I don't know what he's up to?
He has something I want?
I don't trust him?
I don't like him?
I'm afraid of him?
I hate him?

10.
Not even a leaf moving. Check the back seat:
it's empty. You get in. Driving the right roads: busy,
but not congested. Driving not too fast, not
too slowly. All the doors locked.
It's the end of the century.
You just want to get home.

Your Bird

Not just confined like a parakeet, no, it is *trapped*
and frantic, a wild bird, charging itself against the cage
(a space too small for it to stretch its wings),
losing a couple of downfeathers, which flutter—
                                        silent, though:
holding its breath to hear its heartbeat better—
You take the cage away *(it's wrong for a live thing
to be kept from its habitat)*
                            but the bird won't fly, either:
it preens its feathers, as if it were killing time . . .
You want it to take off: the cliché, *free as a bird,*
the typical picture—a winged silhouette on the wind,
a raptor's shadow as it scans the ground—
the bird extends one wing, shakes itself, raises
its claw to its breast (it is no predator; is, potentially,
prey);
        and in the end you put your hand out to it:
a possible safe foothold—will the bird be lifted
to the window, will it determine from there
a trajectory you could follow, if just with your eyes?

Adopted Bird

In his cage at the back of the house, the adopted African Grey talks to him-
self. Repeats phrases he learned before his previous owners divorced. "You
always say that." "I do not." "Bitch!" "No! No! No!" In the next room, a
woman listens. She thinks of her coworker, the woman who sold her the bird,
as she listens again and again to the marital fight. *No! No! Get out of here!* The
bird has that woman's voice down cold, she thinks.

Departures

How many thousands of years ago it left (or tried to leave;
this one didn't make it), the little proto-camel that used to stand
in the Albuquerque airport, I don't recall,
but—*Camelops hesternus*—remember *that*, formal title
of a beast exhumed at Ghost Ranch, bone by bone: reassembled,
placed frail and silent in its own glass box as if to say, "You want departures?
Here's a departure . . ."
                              Go ahead, ask a paleontologist:
ancestors of camels roamed the west before they walked away
over the isthmus to Asia. True fact. —But worse,
there's a brand-new airport now and no one knows
what happened to the skeleton . . .
                                        How many times goodbye?
Migrated, dead, extinct, resurrected, lost—each time
the ribs and pelvis, the long bowl of the head
hitchhike their way back home, the open jaw
mouthing its years-late greeting: *Remember? Sure you do!*
—spelling its last name out, palming the sepia pictures
where both of you grin at the camera. *That's not me,*
you protest, squinting at your own face. —But it is.

Landscape Duel

—the northwoods mounting its offensive:
white birches in the late light of early afternoon
glowing bare, the winter sky brilliant, the air
(unbreathably cold) taken in through the wool weft
and fleece of a scarf, the lake dramatic, steaming: and I want
the woods to win (my newest darling) though it was I
who carried the mountains with me, carried
the desert of sage and chamisa here, the wide sunsets
ruddy against the pastel distance,
and who fueled their counterattack with my faithfulness.
And what of the ocean from childhood, and the city
with its rectangular stone trunks and massifs, its heaven
of spires? I was true to each of them, girded them,
armed them all, and set them against the others.
Now in the night they wish to know who
I love best, like siblings beleaguering
their passionate mother: in the sleepless dark
the stars are suddenly bright, a rescue party
coming upon me from afar, their torches
lit and flickering across the miles—

Still Life with Bad Dog

An azure-glazed pitcher; a few breakfast peaches; poppy blooms;
Matisse's empty easel, akimbo; tourists loitering in the room . . .

An aftermath of argument: harrowingly calm, night
inscribes its farewell note and hides it somewhere in the room.

For weeks someone breathed threatening messages to my machine
which I kept and played back to myself, evenings, in my room.

So many rejected dresses thrown aside as she packed: they floated
down to the bed and puddled in chairs after she left the room.

Coming home late I found the down pillow gutted and shaken,
furring with its soft innards every surface in the room.

Drive Shaft

On my back on a gravel road in the far north I learned to remove the drive shaft from an old Jeep. This is the lesson: you never know what may soon become inessential. The universal joint sheared off, and the drive shaft scraped sparks on the ground. A passing motorist thought to help me: he'd seen me with the drive shaft in my hand. "I don't need help," I said. I put the drive shaft in the back seat. I would put the Jeep in four-wheel drive, and the truck would pull with its front wheels. "I'm just getting rid of this drive shaft," I told him. "Women and cars," he muttered, shaking his head.

Post-Solstice

Here is the slippery bargain: every day a sliver more light, a tiny
margin of sun to give us hope: *they are lengthening, see:*

in exchange for the fifth-snowiest winter in history
and every day a record-setting low: zero this morning,
windchill minus fifteen or twenty—*it's better today—*

and the scientists of global warming have deferred
to their colleagues who tout a new Ice Age, glaciers and all.

Talking cold business in the café
with men who fix cars and admire our gear: *I need
a pair of snowshoes like that there*

*to get in to this hunting lodge I got off Highway 2
'bout a mile from any access road,
my old ones don't do me no good—*

and then about the backcountry where moose like to go,
bow-hunting tales, getting lost in the white terrain,

finding the nineteenth-century homestead that still had its roof
and a grand piano inside: *folks had to get out in a hurry*

—why else leave it? No trails there now,
it's more or less lost, way too remote, the snow

drifting through the glassless windows, dry as pollen, creatures
sheltering in the magnificent box—*Next time I run into it,*

maybe I'll go in, play a tune, he says, thick fingers twitching
a remembered lesson against the china mug. The other

slaps his tip on the stained formica: checks his watch:
Damn! he says mildly, stretching as if waking:

here it is five o'clock and still light!

The Bachelor's House

The couple buys the house, knowing the work it promises
is mostly simple labor:
                              scouring a tub that seems
never to have been washed; taking up the foul carpets and paying someone
to haul them away. They won't be surprised by a bad roof,
rewiring: he's already checked those out,
                                          while she, there in the kitchen,
found the bright compensation of a pristine oven, its window
thick with years-old dust—

it was the worst of those they bid on, and told
most about its lowering bachelor owner, hairy and taciturn
at the closing, smelling of machine oil—

she wonders whether he, the man who lived here, had a greater
or lesser tolerance for loneliness
                                    than the bachelor who labelled
everything in sight in his crooked script, who rode a mower
twice-weekly over his acre lot, whose closets (opened wide by the proud realtor)
stockpiled soap and tissues against a year of crisis,
whose cupboards held seven boxes of cereal
designated with the days of the week:
                                      was he, being busy, less lonely
or more so, craving an audience for his order?

(In college, her friend stored his clean laundry
                                          out in the open room,
the folded piles of tee shirts, balled-up socks pyramided on his dresser,
on display;
            while within the drawers he hid his soiled clothes. *More logical,* he said,
than finding dirty socks all over the place—

and maybe this was a sign, like early symptoms of inherited disease
beginning to show themselves in small, unalarming ways:
                                                      a slight cough,
forgetfulness?)
                Soon they will sand the floors to the gold oak grain

21

(did he ever marry? she's trying to remember)
                                        and do something about the light,
or lack of it, in the bedroom she'll use for a study.

(Two old Norwegian brothers in her hometown
walked each other daily around the block,
                                one (younger) propping the other up
by a meager arm, making a caterpillar's progress;

and then one day they weren't there;
                        and before long
their nieces ordered the series of trailer-sized bins behind the house
and commenced emptying it,

brought three sick cats to the vet for salvaging, tossed
all the unusable furniture, the spoiled fragmentary saved and cherished junk,
and dealt with the rodent problem.)

                        (is he still working for that outfit
in Virginia? she wonders.)

It may be that the bachelor—the seller—spent his days
somewhere else, oblivious of the mess at home and, returning at night,
allowed the house to darken, become comfortable
in its own growing atmosphere of shadow;
                                she likes to think
he couldn't (literally) see it: she does not want
to imagine him actually *living* there (in the house
that is now her house, now *theirs*) being actively neglectful,
slovenly from preference,
                        instead of being tricked into his unkempt life
by the sirens (work? a lover?) that called him away. Better that this be accident
than that he felt
                no disgust with his mildew-crusted bath, that he watched,
approvingly, the scum build and build in the refrigerator and let the cat
mark the ivory carpet—

(she remembers her college friend
making a meal the week before he left. He was using up his provisions,
eating just what he found in his cupboards, buying nothing new
that would then have to be moved:

> a plate of white rice; a can of fruit cocktail
purchased, then forgotten, by a roommate; pimiento-stuffed olives;
saltines—)

All she feels from all these men is loneliness. It seems
resident in the woodwork, denizen of every major appliance:

> *and what,*

she thinks, *if it can't be gotten out, if it's infectious?* She starts
with the windows: vinegar, water, a pile of torn newspapers,
a strong circular motion,

> washing them all first from inside

and then, when those are finished, moving outdoors . . .

The Aquarium

From above her, from the balcony:
>   *Look at that,* she says. *Blue stones.*
Dropping down. Scattering on her tiny apartment patio, naked concrete,
they fall there sometimes, a feral scurry, like a live thing
scrabbling in the walls—
>   blue stones, tame aquarium gravel. The man
upstairs from her scoops from a large bag
>   and some spills over—
I don't go out there now, she says. *You slip on those rocks
you could break a leg. Ambulances, hospitals, forget it.* As for sweeping,
sweeping, sweeping:
>   *he'll only drop more: what does he care?*
It's not his medical bills . . .
Defended from the surging Southern sun with awnings, drapes,
creamy opaque shades all drawn,
>   she leaves home only on Thursdays
when the coupons come out in the paper: *My doctor, dentist, bank, supermarket
all right together, less than a mile to drive*
>   (the highways
are death, she'll tell you: drunks, big trucks, people with guns);
and Thursdays too she treks to the steel wall of doors
that holds her mailbox with its tricky lock:
>   the rest of the week is waiting
and watching TV.
>   These are her family ringing the dinner table,
these her considerate children,
>   whose secrets are hers:
who's in love, who betrayed whom, their complicated relationships;
they are intimate; they are faithful to her,
>   they are not like you, the daughter,
listening in the kitchen as she explains it all, hiding your thoughts,
a tiny cascade of stones in the background,
chittering—
>   the set giving off its changeable light—

The Mortician's Son

I know the wife of a mortician's son. Her husband learned some things growing up, she says, things that had stayed with him. He'd had to wash twelve hearses every Saturday: huge black Cadillacs. They had to gleam before he could play with his friends. Now forty-five, he can wash a car in under ten minutes, she tells me, and polish it better than it looked in its showroom before anyone had ever lived with it or taken it out in the world. Better than new. *He has that gift from his father,* she says.

Hieroglyphs

As it turned out, the artist lived in my old home town
a short drive away, the town I could identify only from a height
of three-and-a-half feet from the floor with my first pointy glasses:
the path I walked to school, to Cory Mooney's; the streets
I wasn't permitted to cross—
                              My husband had met him
at a colony: he painted wild bright abstracts then and drew cartoons
and had a studio in a big city
                                    where we were traveling, now, years later,
admiring the lithographs of letters, postcards, *written things*
done in a comic hieroglyphic, an elaborate hand-done greeking;
he slipped one into an envelope—a wedding present—and took us home
to meet his wife, have lunch . . .
                              When our guests see the lithograph
framed in our house, they often ask what language it is in, what it means,
literally: how it's translated into English, what each symbol
stands for—
            I had my old, child's voice, I enunciated: giving
our old address the same way I'd recited it with my phone number,
my first-middle-last name, for my mother (in case I was lost,
in case the police needed to know)
                                    and the artist knew right where it was:
had done some business with the current owner, a carpenter; it was not far
from his own house. We could drive past:
                                    I recognized at once
where the Caulfields had lived, where Marie and Kathleen across the street
had left each day for Catholic school, the Christopolous place, the Haleys'
greenish stucco—
                  but our house was different: gray paint, a new
boxy third floor put on: unproportional, heretical, the porch swing gone,
but from the alley the backyard just right with its climbable cherry,
the door to the cellar—
                        The lithograph looks like a letter the artist wrote
to a printer along with a sketch of his print, with arrows, instructions
that might say, for example, "bleed," but are instead inscrutable: it isn't
a letter after all—

Of course I craned my neck back as we drove off.
The artist's wife gave us a tour of their house; we walked to a deli
and, graced by late-season bees, ate outdoors in a part of town
I never had seen as a child.
                          There are two ways of looking at that print: you can
squint and get close trying to make out characters one by one, or you can stand
far back and take it all in at once:
                              then the squiggles and figures surprise you
the way some of them seem to come forward, as if offering something—

The Erotics of Detail

The angle his head made to his raised arm in the terminal crowd,
waving as I came off the plane; his insistent use of the term "small *a*"
in math class, when the rest of us said *"little a"*:
                            details I've taken away
from men, storing them back:
                        the way my date cleaned my windshield,
giving the squeegee a good smart shake between the swipes; how he read
to himself, but said the esses out loud:
                            one detail rebuilds the entire time;
remembering eroticizes it:
                        his habit of drinking iced bourbon from a snifter;
the way he turned his hand up, describing a dish he had cooked.
                                        There was
a man whose girlfriend had left for good, who missed the smell
of the soap she used—it had stayed a long time on her pillow—
so he bought some himself, and used it;
                            he washed his towels in it, though
it wasn't *that* kind of soap; he never could make that smell come back,
he said, could never match her *chemistry:*
                            he seemed to think
if he were able to do that much he could bring her back as well,
as if nothing had happened:
                        he told me this as if it were not
the most secret thing in the world, that homemade spellcasting—
                                    but I
don't want those people back: I rather prefer the sudden *frisson* of hearing
someone call somebody "Slick," for example, as he once did to me, and having
that affair crash down again into the present:
                                as if Proust's
madeleine had first been fed to him by a lover: the whole experience changed,
become physical, charged, sexual, visceral:
                                passing:
                                    leaving a residue
of tenderness for the failures that have supplied us with these
interesting scars—

28

The Time Savers

Florida, 1985

None of us knew how to do the tidying-up one does
when somebody dies: family of slow learners, too lucky
and longer-lived than most. We went through
what we hoped were the motions,
holding something high: *What about this?*
Do you want it? —So my mother
could not speak to us for days, except to say
Get rid of it, her cracked voice
poking its hard way out. So Allen,
purging our father's bureau after the funeral,
lifted out shirts bound with their paper strips
back from the laundry for years,
from the week he retired—
clothes with a secret smell
of wood, of unopened drawers—
and found two leather books
smaller than wallets, their green pages
filled with purple writing: *Laird & Lee's*
Diary and Time Saver, with four lines a day
in what was then and occasionally now
might still be called *his hand*:
my father's round and upright hand
clasped in surprise by my own—
with all its secrets, for once,
falling open . . .

Who

—From the obituary

a member of The Tribune editorial staff for 25 years and a prominent author
*

at 83, in Florida
*

*credited with changing national opinion toward Dr. Sam Sheppard in the early
    1960s and helping him receive a new trial*
*

on the best seller list for 14 weeks in 1961
*

*"a fine book because it is an expression of the American conscience, an expression
    of the inquiring mind that refuses to go along with the mob"*
*

a murder mystery novel set at a metropolitan newspaper
*

*executive editor of the Milwaukee Sentinel and later editor in chief of the
    Milwaukee Post*
*

the trial in Dayton of Bugs Moran
*

the Till case in Sumner, Mississippi
*

Survivors include his wife; a son; a daughter; a sister . . .

Particulars

LAIRD & LEE'S DIARY AND TIME SAVER 1920 With 16 Maps in Four Colors Including United States Territorial Acquisitions and four new maps showing the many changes due to the great war.

Concise Chronology of the World War—Handy Reference Tables—Population U.S. and Canadian Cities—Population of U.S. by States—U.S. and Foreign Postage—Telephone Numbers—Cash Accounts and Medical Hints.

Complete Reference Calendar—Business, Civic and Religious Holidays—Astrological Signs for Each Day of the Year—Phases of the Moon, Etc.

TWENTY-FIRST ANNUAL EDITION

Full Name *Paul A. Holmes* [signature practiced several times around the borders of the page]
Residence [the word "College" penned in as a prefix] *310 W. Dayton St., Madison* [crossed out] *621 Milton St.* [crossed out] *701 West Johnson St.*
Business Address [the word "Business" crossed out and replaced with "Home"] *Milton, Wisconsin.*
Name of Firm *Capital Times— B.2200*
My [illegible, inked out] Phone is *Milton— 323 / Madison— Badger 197* [crossed out] *6107*
City, Town, and State *Madison Wis*
My Automobile No. [the word "Automobile" crossed out and replaced with "Ford"] *195,340*
My Height *5' 10"*, Weight *137½*, Complexion *beautiful,* Age *uncertain.*
In case of accident or serious illness please notify *the nearest M.D.*

TWENTY-SECOND ANNUAL EDITION

Full Name *Paul A. Holmes "A.B."*
Residence *701 West Johnson St.* [crossed out] *169 Mason St.*
Business Address *Capital Times Co.* [crossed out] *Milw. Sentinel*

Name of Firm [crossed out; the space is filled with phone numbers] *Home Phone No. B. 6107* [crossed out] *Milton 323 / Broadway 3819*

My Office Phone is *Badger 2200* [crossed out] *Broadway 5000*

City, Town, and State *Wisconsin—Madison*

My Automobile No. [the word "Automobile" crossed out and replaced with "Ford"] *173-049*

My Height *5′10″*, Weight *139*, Complexion *rotten*, Age *uncertain.*

In case of accident or serious illness please notify *the nearest M.D.*

A Box of Old Slides

Endless pockets of change, endlessly fingered:
the chimes of his presence standing late at night,
alone, backlit from the hallway.

———————

My mother brought a puppy home before I was born and became distressed
  because he was little and did not bark. *How would he survive in the world
  with its dangers?*
So it happened that my father found her kneeling before a chair in the living
  room. The puppy sat on the good upholstery watching this woman, not
  yet my mother, yap at him. (The sage and curious look of young dogs.)
  How long did she keep this up? Long minutes: until he got the idea and
  yapped back. Delight—laughter!
She was exactly half his age when I was born, precisely between us.

———————

I sneaked into the room where he napped and curled up next to him,
wrapped both my hands round his large arm. Listened to the catches his
breath made, the rhythm of snores . . .

Odors of cigarettes and after-shave.

———————

"Spending the day with Grampa?" the young man asks me. All white teeth.
(Grampa is nowhere around: why does he ask me this?)
"I'm her *father*," my father explains, and the boy stops smiling.

My mother, fuming: "I can't wait 'til *I'm* seventy: I won't have to give a damn about anybody!"

A door slams.

A house with a trellis. A child stands before it improbably small, as if to provide the scale: a child of two or three years, his hair gathered to the side with a bow and falling past his shoulders in careful curls. The child is to the house as the house is to—what? It is 1904. The child who is my father steadies himself with his hands, his belly round and thrust out, all by himself on the grass.

In his coffin he is untouchable,
emotionless. He'd always been this way,
except that his eyes are closed now
instead of evasive. When as a child I raced to him,
slamming happily into his legs, he settled his hand
(its tremor fluttering the fingers) on my shoulder,
then peeled my body away
and sent me off. Too loud,
too silly, too quick! His gray hair speaks for him
even now on its last pillow.

What

> **fussing (to fuss):** *v.t., v.i.* **1** To visit or escort
> a girl; to date a girl. **2** To neck or spoon. *Obs.*
> See **kick up a fuss.** --**er** *n.* **1** A ladies' man.
> *c1910. Obs.* **2** A girl's date, particularly a col-
> lege girl's date. *Archaic.*
>
> —Partridge, *A Dictionary of Slang*

March 22, 1920. In which due to Jeff's initiative
I fail to spend any money but
nevertheless get most completely
and royally fussed.
March 28, 1920. A rainy dismal Palm Sunday.
Escort the fair Sabina to a
movie. She is slightly adamant.
Women are damned nuisances.
April 3, 1920. The resumption of diplomatic relations
with Elizabeth on a pure status quo ante bellum basis.
Leo & I visit Milton— the flivver flivs—
all is as before Nov. 1 maybe
April 10, 1920. The clan convenes and I step out
the elusive Bessie Badger by a mere
whim of fate. Puncture
the fliv. See Zyda.
May 2, 1920. Details of glorious dinner at "Connie's
Carlton." Retrieve my H.S. ring.
Meet Betty at Y. She is elusive.
Spend evening at home.
He's a month short of nineteen, when he'll write,
"I am as old as I look"—what with
repeated trips from Madison to Milwaukee,
freelancing to the dailies, his regular job,
a full set of classes, and flivvering back to Milton;
what with the throngs of women to be stepped out,
picked up, fussed, nabbed, escorted,
and simply seen. He's the star of a silent movie
in fast jerky black-and-white: a speedy hero

with only occasional grace, living
a nonstop youth . . . now he's a sportswriter,
covering fights between Matsuda ("The Jap")
and Kid Hanson. One week Hanson gets his!
Next week, He trims Matsuda! *The paper*
prints my story. In between
he's cutting classes, pushing all his limits,
knowing better, squeaking by.
Call up Helen and step her out, flivvering hither and yon
aimlessly to poor purpose. Bid her a farewell forever.
So ends another perfectly good woman.
Sometimes they go out dancing in the city.
Sometimes they purchase bootleg liquor, drinking it
outdoors in the open, or in somebody's rented rooms.
They play "Hot Hand" hearts with other couples,
and somebody gets "escorted down the line
for ten berries"; they go see Pola Negri at the Palace,
Eddie Cantor at the Majestic, and he notes down
a second late-night date with a chorus girl. In dreams
does my father guess he'll put off being a father
almost forty more years? Things come
so naturally to him now: the friends, the women,
the easily sold stories, the passing grades.
In October he'll solemnly record the date
Wherein I come the closest I ever came
to losing the irretrievable.
I mark the moment: eight years
before my mother is even conceived, who to this day
is jealous of the women my father loved:
living, dead, and the multitudes of them
he knew before she was old enough to be young
and adventuresome and on her own in Chicago.

Wild Women I Have Known
(Part One)

—From my father's 1921 diary

1. Addene Greene
2. S.O.B. (IKE) Chicago
3. S.O.B. (LARSON) Chicago
4. S.O.B. (BOB) Chicago
5. S.O.B. (JACK) Chicago
6. S.O.B. (Gibney) Chicago
7. Leona Schluffelbein
8. Emily Schluffelbein
9. Bert Freeman
10. Mae Beach
11. Florence Jackson
12. Little Eva
13. Dorothy Merrifield
14. Alice Berger
14½ . S.O.B. Fiddler
15. Catherine Hauser
16. Zyda Mae Price
17. Hattie Bartz
18. Thelma (Jefferson)
19. D. Davis
20. Ethel Boot (Ike)
21. Gertie Wendt
22. S.O.B. (Miller) Wash ave
23. S.O.B. (Miller) Wash ave
24. S.O.B. (Miller) E. Main
25. S.O.B. (Giddings)
26. Elizabeth Cunningham
27. Sabina Lynaugh
28. Bertha Ostand
29. S.O.B. (Geoff) Janesville
30. S.O.B. (Ike) Janes-Edgerton
31. Babe Skelly

32. S.O.B. (Butch) Janesville
33. Elise Hauser (Jefferson)
34. Catherine Hoesly (Jefferson)
35. Edith Diskoff (Jefferson)
36. Babe (S.O.B.) (Butch) Ft. At.
37. Hattie (S.O.B.)
38. S (?)
39. Eulalie (Ulelale)
40. Betty Sheppard
41. Lucille Fergusen
42. Carrol Haessel
43. Louise Morehausen
44. Lydia Kemgiland
45. Margauerite Murray
46. Anne
47. Myrtle
48. Madeline
50. Helen Tomlinson
51. Clara S.O.B. (Leo)
52. Vernalene Johnson
53. Dolly
54. Laura Giltz - (J. Heid)
55. Miss (Fee) Male
56. Hazel Hansel (Chadbourne)
57. Stella Waleski
58. Edna Waleski (409 Wash St)
59. Dorothy Cook
60. Carina Holennbe
61. Grace
62. Mae
63. Helen
64. Clara
65. Lucille
66. Connie Nolan
67. Jewel
68. Helen Ryan
69. S.O.B. (P.C.)
70. Ruth Connoly

72. Molly McKay
73. Anita Fubing
74. Ruth (St. Charles)
75. Marie Keenie
76. Hildegarde Jaeger
77. Flo
78.

Wild Women I Have Known (Part Two)

Roaring Twenties

Off in the Capital City, the women drink moonshine, play cards, and dance in the choruses of traveling variety shows. They allow certain liberties to be taken. O liberty! Smoke drifts through all their doings. Their hair is audaciously short; their skin translucent as vellum. Beautiful women, whose beauty keeps no secrets: their bodies plumper and paler than can be healthy; their expressions giddy with daring. I search my father's scrapbook with its photographs and clippings: round faces with beestung lips. His type? And the decade got named for the sounds the wild make . . .

S.O.B.

I've come to think it isn't what you're thinking. It's a mystery. He'd never have labeled a woman anything's "son"; that was sloppy, unnecessary, inaccurate. Was it that you, Number Two, were *Stepped Out By* Ike? And Number Three, by Larson? Were you both from *South Of the Border* in Illinois? July 1921: "Leo and I step a couple of S.O.B.'s in flivver in p.m." *Stepping-Out Beauties? Sisters Of Brothers? Same Old Birds? Starchy Old Broads?* Nameless women until he begins to name them: Babe. Helen. Clara. *Saw On Business? Stood Out Back? Short Of Breath?* Why does a man's name follow most of these entries? Was he keeping a record of women he might have seen only one evening, of women whose names he'd already mostly forgotten? If so, why was he keeping a record at all?

Forty-nine. Seventy-one. Perhaps they were so distinctive their names could not be spelled out, like that of the Jewish God. Even the numbers he in his coarseness would have assigned them must be obliterated from the list.

Their Names

In the newspaper January first they print a list of the previous year's most popular names for babies, names taken from soap-opera characters, from athletes, actors and musicians. Today they are Courtneys and Ashleys and Caitlins. Back in the twenties, from his random compilation, they were Helens (3) and Dorothys (2). Florences (2, if you count "Flo"). Two Maes, not counting Zyda Mae Price. Two Hatties and two Catherines. Two Babes and two Lucilles. Two Claras. Two Ruths. Sabina. Lydia. Vernalene. Dolly. Hazel.

"I didn't come along until he was 51, and he'd done a lot of living up to then that I didn't get to hear about except in stories." My husband and I listen to this voice in the car as we drive to the woods to ski: a serious woman singer who found the fiddle her daddy played before he got born again. Nobody ever mentioned he'd been a musician. She said her mother thought he'd hidden it because it reminded him of his old life, not because it was evil. We look at each other, both of us from our silent families, and know that in our lives we would never have learned about the days when our fathers played for dances. We'd never have found out what they were like before they were saved.

"Hazel Hansel," she points out to me, "was his first wife." We're still cleaning out the room my father died in; I'm showing her the list I've found in the second diary. I mistakenly believe it will cheer her up. *Look, Mom! Youthful folly!* Hazel Hansel is Wild Woman 56: same as the year I was born. There were first and second wives, Hazel and Virginia, whom I didn't learn about until I was practically grown; this is the first time I've heard Hazel's maiden name. My mother will rage at me later, "Why do you even care?" It hurts her. All of it history before either of us was born.

Who is "the vamp" he meets at the end of 1919, whom he writes about until the following July? Who "the Frosh"? Who "the switchboard queen" who occupies ten months of his notations? Are their real names on his list, or are they even now a secret? Who were the "Male sisters" he and Leo flivvered with to Sun Prairie in July 1921, one of whom he enters into the list as "Miss (Fee) Male"? Who was the "nameless horror" Miller stepped him with? Who, who? And why, indeed, *do* I even care?

I memorized some poems at my father's suggestion when I was little: "I Have a Little Shadow That Goes In and Out With Me," "Christopher Robin kneels at the foot of his bed. . . ." Poems always about little boys. Only one was about a girl, a curious little girl, a naughty girl who asked too many questions. "I keep six honest serving men: they taught me all I knew. Their names are What and Where and When and How and Why and Who," says the disapproving speaker. The little girl, he says, "keeps *ten million* serving men who get no rest at all! She sends them abroad on her own affairs from the second she opens her eyes: one million Hows, two million Wheres, and seven million Whys!" I still have it memorized and I haven't seen it in years. Only recently did it occur to me that the serving men, the useful questions, are the same as those a journalist learns to use in the course of a story. I imagine their names resonating for my father as I chattered on in my child's high voice.

It happens that a few years after his death I go through the legal procedure of taking back my birth name. Though I'd been divorced years before I am still fiddling with my identity. My friend Jane said, "It's all just some damn man's name, anyway"—but she kept her first husband's name through the two marriages that followed and failed. Business reasons, she said. Months pass. My brother, who was always called by his middle name, Allen, announces that he now wants to be called by his first name, Paul. My mother has been Mrs. Paul Holmes as long as I've known her. My brother's son is Paul Allen Holmes. One by one, all of us are returning our names to his.

My Mother's Clown

Before I met your father,
she said, *I dated a clown—*
a professional clown, really, he knew
how to juggle and things, walk on his hands—
the things clowns know—
I remember
he brushed his tongue every day:
he told me he had to keep it
nice and pink,
he was always sticking it out
at children, Children want to see
a clean tongue, *he said—that was one*
of the big rules the clowns had—

Of course I imagined he was always
wearing his clown suit: my mother
arm in arm with Bozo
sashaying down the street: I must have had
the child's uncomprehending
big eyes, trying to parse it,
trying to figure out
why something would be so—

how much *better* to have married
Bozo, of course—what
a question!—what was she
thinking of, settling instead
for the serious,
the black and white, the
difficult, the gone?

Where

He stands in the green Wisconsin summer, humidity packed around him
like so much sodden wool; the incessant nattering insects, the busy grass

whisking them out of its hair; and he in his white dress shirt and tie, creased
   shoes
serviceably polished, wondering why *here,* why *now?* The one time

I saw my father engage with the natural world, he was up to his waist in
   ocean,
elbows drawn back as if to protect his hands from the water and its

brine sting and blessing. It was Florida and he was finished with work.
Did we go only once to the beach as a family, twice, in all the years

we lived there? I'm unsure: I'd reached the age when I didn't want them
   around:
nobody else had parents, it seemed, so how did I get stuck? He was an in-
   doors,

air-conditioned man. He didn't mind if I went there myself with Laura,
walking from Commercial to Sunrise Boulevard, stopping at Howard
   Johnson's

for mint ice cream and a Coke, wearing a bathing-suit top and my un-
   hemmed
faded hip-huggers. Neither of us could lie still on a towel, so we needed

to be going somewhere, restless as hell at fifteen. Commercial to Sunrise
(The Elbo Room), then back again. I feared the ocean every bit as much

as he did . . . But there in northern Wisconsin by the lake, I'd have told you
he was far too citified to stand it in the heat; he'd be cross, damned uncom-
   fortable,

so stiff he couldn't bend his legs, like an angry male Barbie; I'd have sworn
he'd prefer to have stayed in the car or in my head. But he astonishes me,

unpeeling his crisp slacks, his dark-striped tie, his French cuffs like a magician
to reveal used Army clothes (circa the Great War), purchased in Janesville

for a two-week canoe trip northwards of Rice Lake. He's twenty. Each day he
    pencils
a crabbed summation in his diary: *We are left at Barker Lake with canoe. I
    catch 2 fish.*

Camp in mosquito-ridden place. It rains and we get soaked. (Later he inked the
    entries
over, letting the gray ghosts show through.) *We portage the Radisson dam.*

See some Mennonites. Still eating fish! Paddle all day and reach Bruce.
The characteristic parts of my father's body, I've always thought, were

his feet: delicate as an invalid's, uncallused, white, kept in their soft socks
the way the wedding silver lived in its plush wraps in a special chest,

the aristocrats of his flesh. They seemed to wince, set naked on the floor,
and I'd have sworn they'd never been outside . . . The year of my divorce

I camped across Alaska, who'd never read a topo map, who'd never slept
outdoors. I called my mom collect from Inuvik: *I'm at the ends of the earth,*

I told her. She didn't say "You're crazy!" but she worried. Now I wonder
whether I could have shared that trip with him, the way the world

unwrapped itself from the cities for me suddenly. He might have laughed
to see me pitch that first ungainly tent. He might have told me, "Yes, I

used to camp" (and I'd have gasped). I shed, at last, my child's fear of the
    ocean,
my fear of getting lost, and made up for the years of sheltering in suburbs

by hiking wild miles. You could say we took our feet in two directions.
I'd rather think he didn't toss aside the outdoor world, the lakes and woods

of his beginnings, but that life pressed its own seductive claim: the city,
the city desk, the task at hand, the daily bread thing, the daily

morning news . . . *Eventful wading trip down the East Fork.*
We canoe to Bishop Bridge. Back to Barron at 5 and I start for Milton

from Cameron at 7:30. Arrive 7:30. Greet the family. Go to work
in tobacco and work half day. Letter from Sentinel offers job. Wire confirms it.

I cease work and at 5:30 go to Milwaukee. That's the record. God,
I miss my father: driving through Wisconsin, I wonder where the roads

of 1921 have got to; if the green green green insistent woods
are anything like what he'd have remembered; what on earth

persuaded him to leave and not turn back, and,
as if he'd been their lover, now thrown over,

never say a word about those good old times they'd had.

Prostrated over Fiance's Killing

MADISON, Wis., May 30—While indignation is evidenced throughout Madison as a result of the slaying of Carl Jandorf, Wisconsin sophomore, by Policeman Mathew G. Lynaugh, Saul Sinaiko, wealthy coal and wood dealer, tonight announced his intention of spending any necessary sum of money to assure the punishment of the policeman.

Miss Grace Sinaiko, pretty 19-year-old fiancee of the slain student, is prostrated at her home.

The body of Mr. Jandorf was sent to his home at Grand Rapids today, and at the same time two separate investigations were launched into the killing.

Lynaugh, who, it develops, has a record of too free use of his police baton on several occasions, is held on a manslaughter charge at the Dane County courthouse, and, while reserves and militia await any possible call, he has made no effort to be freed after a long conference on the subject with his attorney.

— Chicago Herald and Examiner, Monday, May 31, 1920
(no byline, accompanied by a formal portrait photograph of Grace Sinaiko)

When

May 28, 1920: Grim tragedy on campus.
Due to Leo, I scoop the
Journal by 25 minutes.

May 31, 1920: I go home at 5:10 and
collect $10 berries.
Spurn the fair Elizabeth.
The Chi Herald prints my story.

This will teach me, I thought, what was *grim* to him at eighteen, what *tragedy*
was: and, sure enough,
when I looked it up it was murder, the first in his long career of lurid front-
page stories—Bugs Moran,
mad Ed Gein, Sam Sheppard . . . for once the diarist matched the old man I
remember,
the man who could write a book in a couple of days while I, ten years old,
peeked from my room down the hall
at a profile hunt-and-pecking hot percussion to the hum of a plugged-in
Remington: yes,
he could have scooped the *Journal* as a boy . . . The policeman held for killing
a college kid
shares a name with a girl my father was seeing all spring: Sabina Lynaugh,
Twenty-Seven on his
Wild Woman list *("Escort the fair Sabina to a movie . . ."):* but if the suspect
under arrest
is brother to her, or cousin, quick-tempered uncle or (worst) even her own
unlucky father,
my father wrote down nothing in his diary reflecting on that news, nothing
that shows he marked
the man's last name. This might have been when he found his real vocation
(June 1: I cut school
to attend the inquest), when he first began to think of law school and—why
not?—a big career in Chicago

covering crime, the city's major business. It wasn't when he first decided to
    write—I know that much.
I have the fat scrapbook of his stories, saved weekly as they ran in the
    Janesville paper
with his photo: a serious boy in a serious white collar. He was thirteen, and
    kept the job
three years. (When I was young and bored in the sticky, green, long summer
    days of childhood,
and came to him complaining, he'd present a ream or so of untouched copy
    paper
freshly cadged from the *Trib*, and suggest I write a book, as if I too were
    yearning into print
at such an age . . .) He went from writing stories to the sports page, but some-
    time (when?)
his focus shifted to the life-and-death perplexity of murder, its unknowables
and evidence. And that was when his lifework clicked in place: that was when
he'd steal or wheedle photos for the paper (as, we figure from the *Herald*'s
    telegram
Get photo fiancee tucked in the diary, he did that day: the student meant
to marry the murdered boy peers out at us from the paper oddly serene, con-
    sidering . . .).
It was when he'd drop a girl because he was on a story. In the diary, she's gone
(Sabina is) until December, maybe longer. *December 20: Al & I*
would have stepped out but were spurned by Betty, Leta, Venda, and even Sabina.
Even Sabina! I feel affection for him, rejected fusser, left to scratch his head,
because I know the craftsman he became was never quite as good with flesh
    and bone
as he had been with words. He hadn't learned to make those muscles work,
    the ones that push
the heart wide open: and this was when they first began to fail him. This was
    when
he felt them shudder mutely and collapse, beyond control, beyond his reach,
    inside.

Why

The subtleties of *adulthood*
blew by me: I thought he was four

and then, suddenly, seventy,
having married my mother during the restless stretch

that was what grownups did
when they went to work alone, before the children,

their lives bleak as a section of highway
everyone had to travel. Fathers disappeared and then came home

over and over for years,
and then were old. And when I learned

the value of a decade, well,
who cared? He didn't have it to spend, that kind of time.

He thought I was his sister
at the end, and called me Alice. His body had caved in.

His eyes gave up.
Who wants to be remembered in their

most imperfect persona,
their oldest bones? I'm after his dreaming years,

his twenties: when he translated
all his grave obsessions into love, his pleasures into schemes

to make him rich, and work
to make him famous; when his body had the radiance

that drew new lovers to it
almost without its knowing; where impulse governed care

without regret, and there
were lessons left to learn the hard way, later,

when he aged. He would not
be tired. He would talk into the late-night smoke

hiding nothing. Let me make—
against my memory of him: too fragile, nursing a bourbon, neat,

up late in his writing chair, facing
the window that opened out on the blackened street—

a young man of my father,
imperfect and impulsive, complete with the grand visions

he'd disclose, drunk
and indiscreet, to whatever wild woman waited up

or waited out the evening.
Let me think of him for once as agile, bright, and reckless,

angling toward her
breathless in the dark.

How

With his Parker 51 fountain pen made in Janesville,
    its black bullet-shaped body, its gold cap. With the heavy
    gunmetal gray Remington electric, its green high-rising keys
    each with a loud report, its hum when it got going
    shaking the tinny table, setting up
    sonorities of labor, of words relentless
    in their midnight attack.

With her hidden violin tucked in its green scarf,
    waiting in its case for the children
    to be born, raised, and sent away;
    waiting to be taken up again,
    to sing. With the bow, the rosin,
    the rest she used for her chin.
    The metronome lost somewhere.

With the black Quink bottle where the pen was filled,
    and with the slurping ink pumping into it.
    With the grainy disc of eraser fastened to its stiff brush.

With music books; with the green paisley scarf
    thrown backwards over her shoulder, a cushion
    for the instrument.

And with all his notes, round script in blunt pencil,
    and the impulse to get it all down;
    with bylines pasted in the scrapbook, and later
    folded into the front. With mucilage stains on the pages.
    (The newsprint cracks where the folds fall. Crumbles.)

With one reporter and one musician
    and the gifts they once brought forward,

separately, for the child.